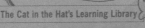

The editors would like to thank
LAURENT MONTESI, PhD,
Department of Geology, Geodynamics Group,
University of Maryland,
for his assistance in the preparation of this book.

Visit us on the Web!
Seussville.com
rhcbooks.com

Educators and librarians, for a variety of teaching tools, visit us at RHTeachersLibrarians.com

Library of Congress Cataloging-in-Publication Data is available upon request.
ISBN 978-1-9848-2971-9 (trade)—ISBN 978-1-9848-2972-6 (lib. bdg.)

MANUFACTURED IN CHINA

10 9 8 7 6 5 4 3 2 1

First Edition

Random House Children's Books supports the First Amendment and celebrates the right to read.

e Lavas I nat Flow!

by Todd Tarpley

illustrated by Aristides Ruiz and Joe Mathieu

The Cat in the Hat's Learning Library®

Random House 🏠 New York

What erupts from below,
spitting fire and gases?
What gurgles with lava
that flows like molasses?

I'm the Cat in the Hat,
and I'm here to explain-o
some marvelous facts
all about the volcano!

Perhaps you are thinking,
"As everyone knows,
volcanoes are mountains
from which lava flows."

But that is not all!

There is more you must see!

Let's explore some volcanoes.

Come on! Follow me!

8

A volcano's a hole
in the earth, did you know?
It allows heat and gas
to escape from below.

Earth is quite hot
underneath its cool crust,
so it must release heat
from its mantle. It must!

Volcanoes allow it
a place to expel
hot lava and ash clouds
and gases that smell.

9

There is more than one type
of volcano. It's true!
Come take a look.
I will show some to you!

A Stratovolcano
has steep sloping sides,
a small, narrow crater,
and thick lava slides.

STRATOVOLCANO

This Cinder Cone type
is quite small and less steep.
Its crater is wide,
but it's not very deep.

CINDER CONE VOLCANO

The odd Shield Volcano
is flat and quite wide.
Lava flows farther
away down its side.

SHIELD VOLCANO

This Lava Dome looks
like a thick blob of tar.
Its lava's too thick
to erupt very far.

LAVA DOME

Each volcano is different.
No one's like the rest.
No one is the worst,
and no one is the best.

This massive one here,
near a town called Pompeii,
erupted quite suddenly
one autumn day.

MOUNT VESUVIUS
NAPLES, ITALY

Big stones and hot ash
were spewed up miles high.
They buried Pompeii
as they rained from the sky.

For seventeen centuries,
Pompeii remained
buried, forgotten,
its fate unexplained.

Today we can visit
the ruins of the town,
while high overhead
the volcano peers down.

13

This volcano is Etna.
It is not small at all.
Compared to Vesuvius,
it is TWICE as tall!

Etna is active.
It blows now and then.
It could blow anytime,
but you never know when.

MOUNT ETNA
SICILY, ITALY

Now people ski down it.

(Seems strange, but it's true!)

I might like to try it someday.

How 'bout you?

The great Mount St. Helens
in Washington State
had a beautiful face
till it met its sad fate.

Off blew its top!
And off blew its side!
It left a big crater
at least a mile wide!

Underneath Yellowstone
National Park,
there's a Supervolcano
that still leaves its mark.

It hasn't erupted for
thousands of years.
And won't again anytime
soon, it appears.

But the mantle below it,
where magma is found,
still heats water that spouts
from a hole in the ground.

YELLOWSTONE CALDERA
WYOMING, UNITED STATES

A Supervolcano
is super, indeed:
gargantuan, massive,
gigantic—agreed!

When Mount Pinatubo
erupted one day,
most of its crater
was blasted away.

MOUNT PINATUBO
LUZON, PHILIPPINES

Within a few weeks
big rains came, and then—
there was a new lake
where its crater had been.

Mount Krakatoa

was strange as can be.

It erupted, then quickly

sank into the sea!

MOUNT KRAKATOA
SUNDA STRAIT, INDONESIA

The eruption?

Among the most powerful ever!

Has any volcano

since beat it? No, never!

Many volcanoes
rise up very high,
but their tops never reach
an inch into the sky.

You may wisely ask, then,
"Just how could that be?"
Well, the tips of their tops
are deep under the sea!

If you think THAT'S amazing
(well, trust me, you ought'er),
did you know MOST volcanoes
are under the water?

If you ever go walking
down by the South Pole,
you may see Mount Erebus
during your stroll.

MOUNT EREBUS
ROSS ISLAND, ANTARCTICA

Edinburgh Castle sits
high on a brink
that is a volcano.
(Thank goodness, extinct!)

On the isle of Hawaii
this huge one is found.
It's called Mauna Loa.
It's flat and it's round.

MAUNA LOA
HAWAII, UNITED STATES

31

There are also volcanoes
in space, did you know?
Four hundred alone
on a moon called Io.

JUPITER

Io

Orbiting the
planet Jupiter

A drum roll now, please,
for we're nearing the end.
Here's the biggest volcano
we know of, my friend.

On the planet called Mars
there exists a volcano
so big that you'd say
if you saw it, "No way—no!"

OLYMPUS MONS

MARS

72,000 FT

MOUNT EVEREST
NEPAL/CHINA
29,029 FT

MAUNA KEA
HAWAII
33,500 FT*

*20,000 FT IS
below sea level

← OLYMPUS MONS IS 350 MILES →
ACROSS AT THE BASE, AND
IT IS SO TALL IT BASICALLY
STICKS OUT OF MARS'S ATMOSPHERE!!!

It's two times as high
as the highest on Earth.
It's not very steep
but has quite a wide girth.

Now, we've seen with volcanoes
the bad they can do—
but there are also GOOD things.
I'll now name a few.

VAPOR

CLOUDS

PRECIPITATION

Volcanoes release
so much vapor—y'know—
that without them we wouldn't have
rain, sleet, or snow!

No puddles, no lakes,

no oceans or rivers!

Not even an ice cube!

(That gives me the shivers.)

They help keep Earth cool,
and here's something quite grand—
volcanoes can actually help
CREATE land!

In fact, many places
were formed thanks to lava:
Hawaii, Tahiti,
Sumatra, and Java.

HAWAII

SUMATRA

PACIFIC
OCEAN

TAHITI

JAVA

39

Now that we know
what volcanoes can do,
I have a question
I'd like to ask you.

Of all the volcanoes
we've seen here today,
which one is your favorite?
How come, would you say?

Take your time. Think about it.
But I'd sure like to know.
Until then, I suppose,
I'll just go with the FLOW.

GLOSSARY

Ash: Fragments of rock created during a volcanic eruption.

Crater: A hole created in the top of a volcano when it erupts. A crater can also mean a hole in the ground created by an impact, like a meteorite.

Crust: The outer layer of Earth, including the oceans, continents, and all living things.

Erupt: How a volcano ejects lava, ash, and gases.

Expel: To eject or push out.

Girth: The measurement around the middle of something.

Habitat: A natural environment for plants and animals.

Lava: Very hot liquid rock emitted during a volcanic eruption. When it cools, it hardens into rock.

Mantle: The layer of Earth beneath the crust where magma comes from.

Massive: Very big.

Molasses: A thick, dark brown syrup made from sugar and used in cooking.

Ruins: The remains of old houses and buildings.

Spew: Erupt very powerfully.

Vapor: Fog, mist, or steam that rises from the ground and stays low in the air.

FOR FURTHER READING

Pompeii . . . Buried Alive! by Edith Kunhardt, illustrated by Michael Eagle (Random House Books for Young Readers, Step into Reading, Step 4). An easy-to-read account of the eruption of Mount Vesuvius and the discovery centuries later of the buried town of Pompeii. For grades 2 and up.

Volcano Dreams: A True Story of Yellowstone by Janet Fox, illustrated by Marlo Garnsworthy (Web of Life Children's Books). A lyrical picture book tour of Yellowstone National Park and the sleeping volcano deep in the ground below. For kindergarten and up.

Volcano: The Eruption and Healing of Mount St. Helens by Patricia Lauber (Simon & Schuster Books for Young Readers). Illustrated with photographs, this award-winning picture book follows the 1980 eruption of Mount St. Helens and the return to life of surrounding plants and animals. For grades 2 and up.

Volcanoes by Seymour Simon (Smithsonian). Written by an award-winning science writer, this picture book introduction to volcanoes is illustrated with fantastic photographs. For kindergarten and up.

INDEX